Supply List

Here's a list of items used for the crafts in this book. All are available at craft stores.

buttons	fabric glue	removable tape
card stock	Glue Dots	ribbon
cord	glue stick	scissors
craft glue	jewelry hardware	seed beads
craft paint	paper	sewing needles
double-stick tape	pencil	thread

button basics

Get to know the buttons used in this book.

Sew-Through Buttons

These familiar buttons come with two or more holes punched out in the middle so that they easily can be sewn onto fabric.

Shank Buttons

Instead of having holes like a sew-through button, a shank button has a hard loop on the back. This allows you to sew on the button without the thread showing. Shank buttons often come in fun shapes and themes, such as animals, toys, and food.

Bubble Buttons

Bubble buttons look just as they sound—like bubbles! They are round and have a loop at the back so that they can be sewn on clothing or strung on a cord. They often look like glass but can be made of plastic.

simple sewing steps

Learn the no-knot method of button sewing.

1. Cut an 18-inch piece of thread. Fold the thread in half and thread both ends through the eye of the needle, making a loop.

2. With the button on the fabric, send the needle from back to front, but don't pull the loop all the way through.

3. Send the needle back through the hole in the button from front to back, and then through the loop. Pull taut.

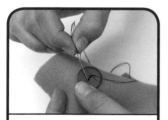

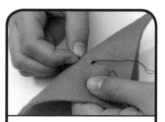

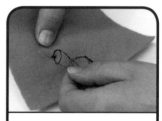

4. Continue sewing through the front and back of the button holes until the button feels secure.

5. With the needle pulled through to the back of the fabric, slip the needle under the sewn stitches, creating a loop.

6. Send the needle through the loop twice and pull taut. Trim off the excess thread.

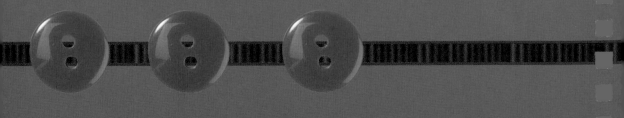

8

wear it

button tops

Buttons can change the look of a shirt. Play around with all kinds of colors and shapes of buttons to find a look you like. You can decorate along the seams or scatter buttons in your own pattern. When you're pleased with your design, sew on each button with a needle and thread or secure it with fabric glue.

shoe jewelry

you will need
- shoes
- buttons
- craft glue or Glue Dots
- clip-on earring hardware

Dress up plain slip-ons or sneakers with cool shoe jewelry. Layer various shapes and sizes of buttons using Glue Dots or craft glue. When glue is dry, attach the buttons to the flat side of an earring clip. Make a second version that matches the first, or use coordinating buttons for a funkier look. When the clips are dry, wear them on your shoes or shoelaces.

sew-sweet socks

If you have to wear knee socks with a school uni-form, or if you just want to give an outfit a twist, a pair of button-embellished socks can show your style. Use the Simple Sewing Steps on page 7 to add buttons to the sides of your sock cuffs. Shank buttons work great and come in fun shapes. Or layer different-colored buttons to create a look that is completely unique.

dress it up

beauty barrettes

Give your hair more style by adorning your 'do with button-beautiful barrettes. Decorate a plain barrette by gluing on layers of buttons. If using craft glue, let each layer of buttons dry before adding more.

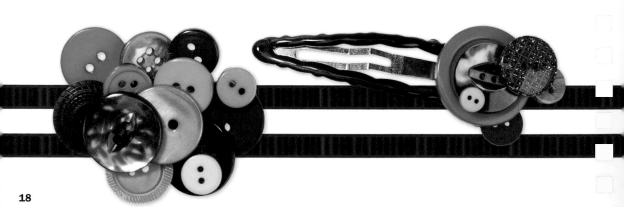

button bangles

Bangle bracelets come in many shapes and colors, but you can make yours even more fashionable with buttons. Glue on one size and color of buttons all around the bracelet, or mix up the buttons for an interesting design.

TIP: Sometimes the buttons will slide off the bracelet before the craft glue dries. Stop this from happening by putting removable tape over the buttons while the glue is drying.

bobby blooms

Dress up a bun or hold back your bangs with a blooming bobby or two. Just slide a shank button onto a fancy bobby pin and pin it into your hair.

22

button stack ring

Coming in sizes fit for the finger, buttons are just right to make into rings. Start by sewing a stack of layered buttons together. You can also add a seed bead as the very top layer. With help from a parent, hot glue the buttons onto a plain ring band and let dry.

you will need

- ⭐ adult's help
- needle
- thread
- scissors
- buttons
- seed bead (optional)
- glue gun & hot glue
- plain ring band

23

easy earrings

you will need
- adult's help
- buttons
- craft glue or Glue Dots
- earring hardware
- needle (optional)
- thread (optional)
- scissors (optional)
- pliers (optional)

Just about any kind of button can be used to build a cool pair of earrings. For post earrings, use craft glue or Glue Dots to layer buttons onto plain earring hardware. Or put posts you already own through the holes of two separate buttons and wear them without gluing.

If you want earrings that dangle, sew a layer of buttons together. Ask a parent to help you hook on earring wires and crimp closed with pliers.

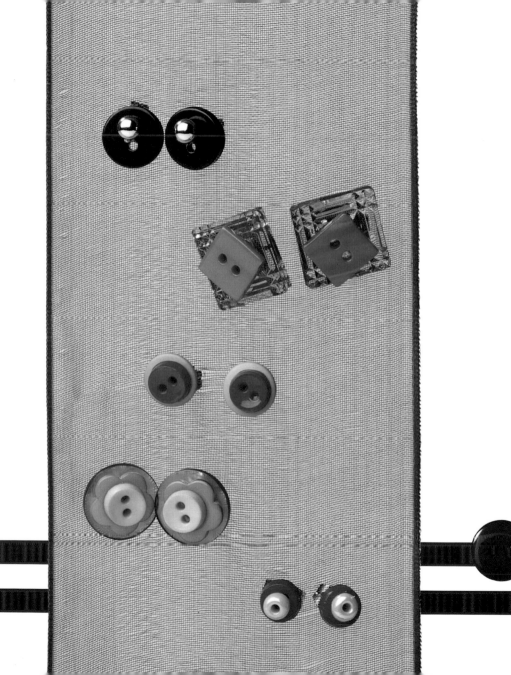

button bag

you will need
- pencil
- purse/bag
- paper
  (optional)
- buttons
- fabric glue

If you think making a collage is only about using paper, think again! Because buttons come in so many colors and sizes, they are fun to use for creating your own shapes and pictures. To decorate a tote bag, use a pencil to lightly draw a shape onto a canvas bag. (You may want to do your sketch first on paper.) Fill in the drawing with buttons. Once you have them laid out the way you like, glue them down one by one with fabric glue. Let the first layer dry before adding more.

animal necklace

Combine button shapes to make all kinds of fun animal faces. Use a flat-front shank button as your animal face base. Layer different-sized buttons to make eyes or snouts, and use square or triangle buttons for ears. Decorate with paper for flat details. Add dimensional craft paint for any 3-D details smaller than a button; let dry. String a cord through the back of the shank. Ask a parent to tie the necklace on for you or help you add jewelry hardware to the ends.

bubble necklace

Use bubble buttons for a really beautiful—and easy-to-make—necklace! Start by cutting an 18-inch length of cord. String on bubble buttons in any color combination you like. You should use at least 4 buttons. String both ends of the cord through the last button to pull all the buttons together. Tie a knot above the last button. Ask a parent to tie the necklace on for you or help you add jewelry hardware to the ends.

button chain

you will need

- 20-inch piece of 1-mm stretch jelly cord
- two-hole sew-through buttons
- seed beads
- scissors

1. Tie a double knot around a bead at one end of the cord. String the cord through a hole in a button. String on a seed bead, and thread the cord through the second hole.

2. Slide the button and bead to the end of the cord. Continue adding buttons and beads. The buttons will alternate facing up and down.

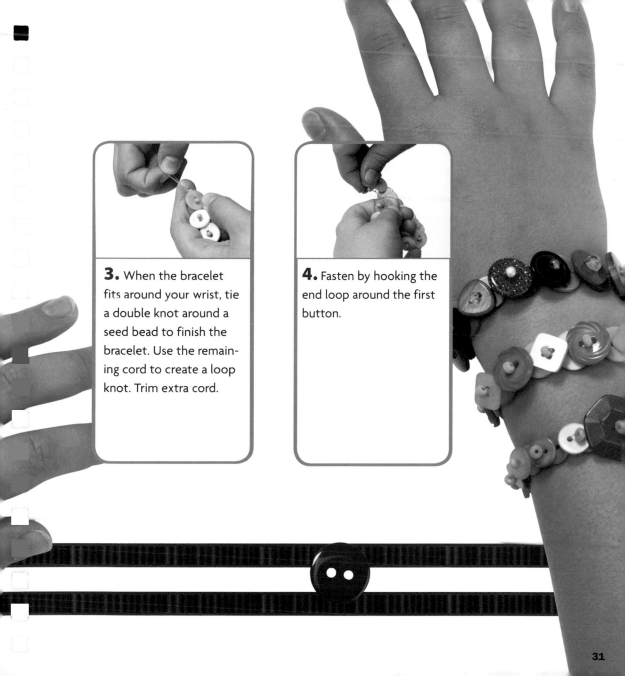

3. When the bracelet fits around your wrist, tie a double knot around a seed bead to finish the bracelet. Use the remaining cord to create a loop knot. Trim extra cord.

4. Fasten by hooking the end loop around the first button.

decorate it

cute cushions

you will need
- throw pillows
- buttons
- fabric glue

Give your bed a blast of style by decorating throw pillows with buttons. Any kind of pillow can be decorated. Just attach buttons in fun designs using fabric glue. Come up with your own designs, or follow the pillow's pattern.

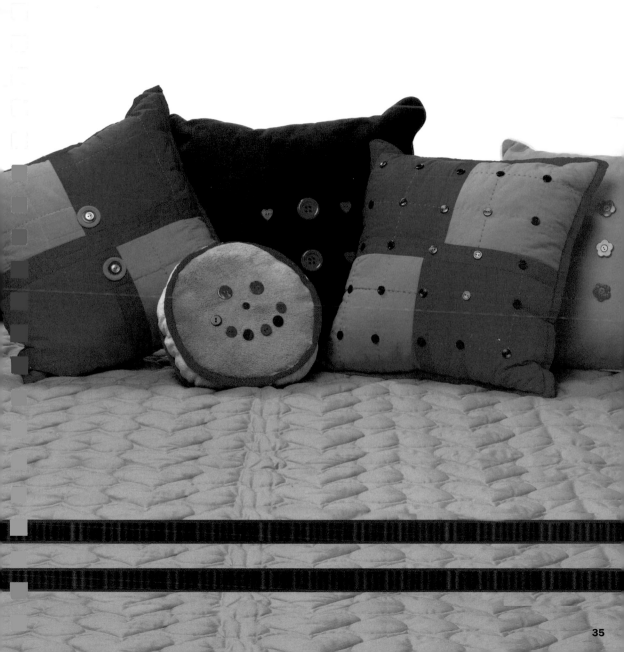

art station

you will need

- cleaned-out jars and tins
- ribbon
- scissors
- buttons
- craft glue or Glue Dots

Get creative with a desk set made just for art supplies. Decorate cleaned-out jars and candy tins with ribbon. Then attach coordinating buttons, layering them in different patterns.

lovely lamp shade

you will need
- plain lamp shade
- ribbon
- scissors
- buttons
- fabric glue

Brighten up your space with a pretty decorated lamp shade. Use fabric glue to attach ribbon and buttons in random patterns, or create shapes such as flowers and hearts.

on/off buttons

you will need
- plain light-switch plate
- ribbon
- scissors
- buttons
- double-stick tape
- craft glue or

Flip on the switch for style! Cover a plain light-switch plate with ribbon and buttons to match your room. Use double-stick tape to secure the ribbon and craft glue or Glue Dots to attach the buttons.

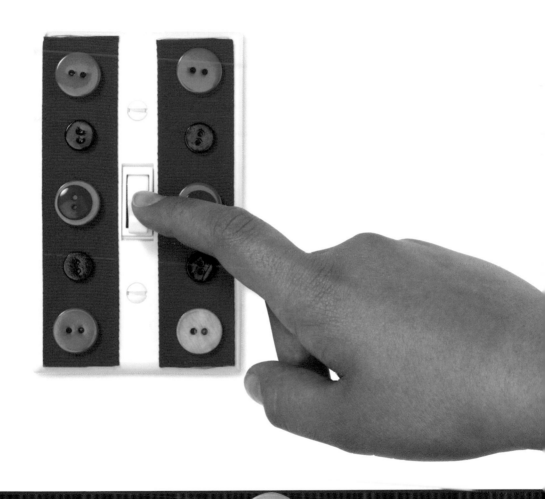

41

creative clips

you will need
• paper clips
• buttons
• craft glue

Paper clips don't have to be boring! With a dab of craft glue and some lightweight buttons, you can hold your papers together with pizzazz.

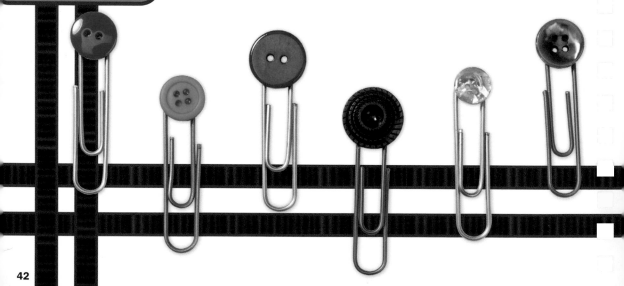

bulletin buttons

Dress up your bulletin board with button-covered tacks. Just use craft glue or Glue Dots to attach buttons to tacks and let dry.

you will need
- ✋ adult's help
- craft glue or Glue Dots
- buttons
- tacks

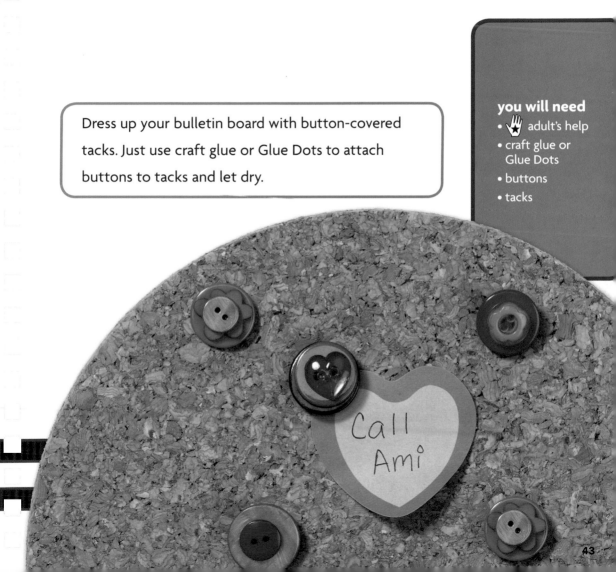

Call Ami

43

picture perfect

A photographic memento will be even more treasured in a fantastic-looking frame. Create your very own pattern using a variety of buttons. Use craft glue to secure; let dry before adding another layer.

trendy trash

you will need
- wastebasket
- buttons
- craft glue
- removable tape
  (optional)

A wastebasket doesn't have to look like garbage. Give it a clean look by using dabs of craft glue to attach buttons that match your room. Let dry.

TIP: Sometimes the buttons will slide off the wastebasket before the craft glue sets. Stop this from happening by using removable tape over the buttons until the glue is dry.

46

give it

button greetings

you will need
- paper
- buttons
- scissors
- Glue Dots
- glue stick
- stickers
  (optional)
- ribbon
  (optional)

Buttons are great for giving dimension to flat gift tags and greeting cards. Use buttons as leaves on a tree, flowers in bloom, or the sun shining in the sky. Or use buttons to create fun and interesting designs that enhance the paper pattern. It's all about being creative!

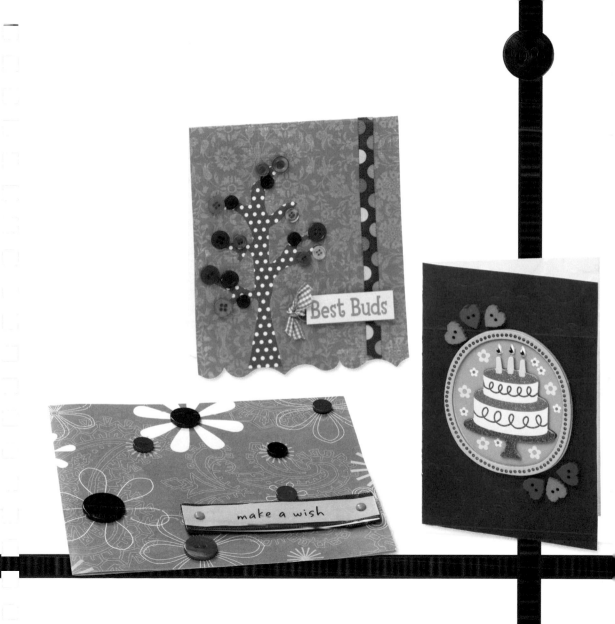

button bags

you will need
- paper gift bags
- decorative paper
- buttons
- scissors
- Glue Dots
- glue stick
- stickers *(optional)*
- ribbon *(optional)*

Change a plain paper bag into a decorative gift bag. With a few buttons, glue, pretty paper, and a little imagination, you'll have a wonderful way to present a present.

cool key chain

1. Create one stack of buttons for a single-stack key chain, or two matching stacks for a double-stack key chain. Cut a piece of thread about 18 inches long. Fold the thread in half and thread both ends through the eye of the needle, making a loop.

2. Sew through a single stack, but don't pull the loop all the way through. Send the needle back through the holes in the buttons and then back through the loop. Pull taut.

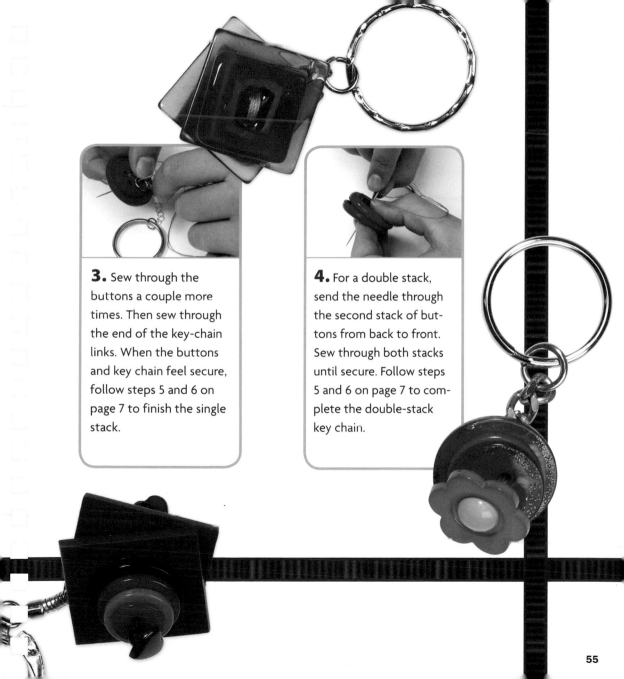

3. Sew through the buttons a couple more times. Then sew through the end of the key-chain links. When the buttons and key chain feel secure, follow steps 5 and 6 on page 7 to finish the single stack.

4. For a double stack, send the needle through the second stack of buttons from back to front. Sew through both stacks until secure. Follow steps 5 and 6 on page 7 to complete the double-stack key chain.

theme tins

Decorated candy tins are great gifts all on their own or with little surprises tucked away inside. Cover the top of a cleaned-out candy tin with paper. Glue on buttons to create a theme. For example, for the dog lover, decorate a tin with puppy and bone buttons. Since shank buttons won't lie flat, Glue Dots are a good way to keep them attached.

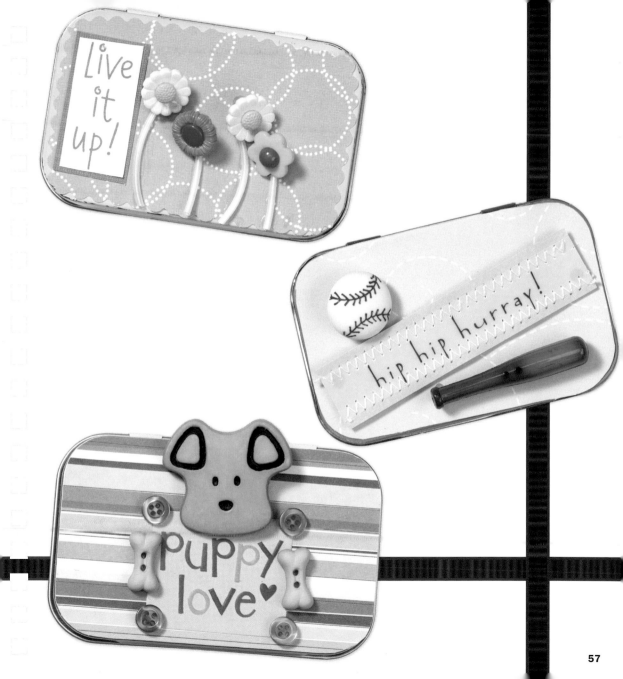

live
it
up!

hip hip hurray!

puppy
love ♥

unique ornaments

you will need
- ✋ adult's help
- plain ball ornaments
- buttons
- craft glue or Glue Dots
- embellishments *(optional)*
- ribbon

Spread some holiday cheer with handmade ornaments. Glue buttons to the outside in different patterns, or fill an ornament with an assortment of different buttons. If the opening of an ornament has sharp edges, ask an adult for help.

forever flowers

To make the flower shank blossoms, slide two or three groupings of sew-through buttons onto a chenille stem. If button holes are large, you may need to bend the stem slightly to prevent sliding. This will give the stem a loopy look. At the top of the stem, slide on a flower shank button, and curl the top of the stem over and back into the button beneath the shank button.

To make the paper flowers, copy the templates on page 62 and trace onto card stock. Cut them out and attach buttons with craft glue or Glue Dots. When dry, glue a chenille stem onto the back of each flower. If the chenille stem sags, twist a second stem together with the first.

flower patterns

Use these flower patterns for the Forever Flowers on pages 60 and 61. To use, photocopy them at 100%.

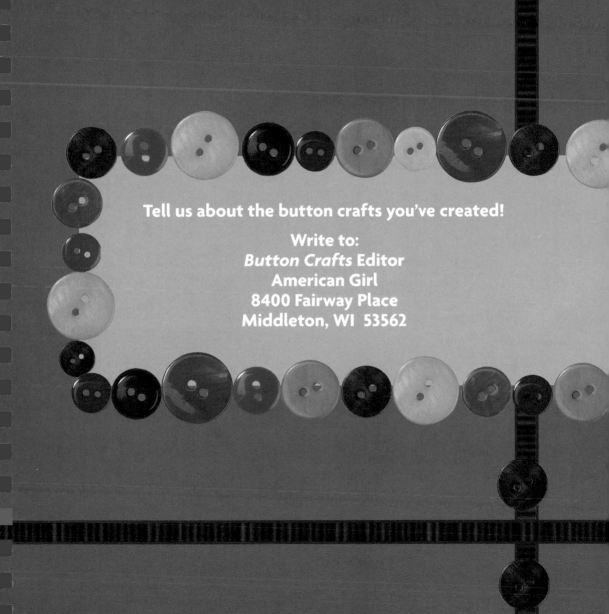

Tell us about the button crafts you've created!

Write to:
Button Crafts Editor
American Girl
8400 Fairway Place
Middleton, WI 53562

Here are some other American Girl books you might like:

❑ I read it.

❑ I read it.

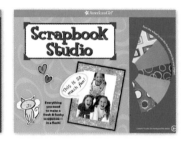

❑ I read it.

❑ I read it.

❑ I read it.